Exploring the threatened oceans

A black-tipped reef shark.

You can see many ocean creatures in the new giant aquariums. It's a good way to feel yourself part of the ocean.

Contents

A world of water and life 4

The open ocean 6

Coral reefs 8

Threats to reef life 10

The cold ocean 12

Underwater forests and meadows 14

Whales, dolphins and seals 16

Sharks 18

Life with a soft body 20

Life in a shell 22

Octopuses 24

Ocean birds 26

Pollution and the ocean 28

Try these 30

Glossary and Index 32

Look up the **bold** words in the glossary on page 32 of this book.

A world of water and life

Perhaps we should call our planet 'Water', rather than 'Earth', because nearly three quarters of its surface is covered by **oceans**.

We live on the crowded land part of the Earth, but four out of every five living things on Earth live in the oceans.

We know most about life on land, yet the first life did not start on land, but in the oceans three billion years ago.

We know that rainforests are places crowded with life, but actually some parts of the oceans have far more kinds of living thing than anywhere on land.

We look at the oceans and they seem immense. Yet, just as on land, all living things are connected. If we harm some, countless others will suffer, including ourselves, for we get almost a fifth of our food from the oceans.

So, let's find out about the oceans, and how to look after them...

Did you know... ?

- The ocean has the tallest mountains in the world and the deepest valleys.
- The ocean isn't just wide, it's deep – 4,000 m deep on average.
- The deepest place in the ocean is the Mariana Trench. It is 11 km deep (7 miles) – that's deeper than Mt Everest is high.

A grouper patrolling a reef.

What does this fish need to stay alive?

The open ocean

Blacktip reef shark

All most of us know about the sea is the coastline. We might play on the beach and paddle in the waves on the beach, but out of sight lie vast areas of ocean where you cannot see land in any direction and where storms raise waves as tall as buildings.

We call this the open ocean. But this ocean is not all the same. Near the surface there is light enough to see easily and plants can grow here.

If you go deeper there is a 'twilight zone' where there is not enough light for plants to grow.

Deeper still is the 'midnight zone' – so deep no light ever reached it.

The deeper you go under the water the more it presses in on your body – this is called water pressure. It also gets colder and colder as you go down. So at the bottom of the ocean it is not only dark but close to freezing and the water pressure would squash us flat!

Stomiatoid fish

Blue lanternfish

Hatchetfish

Spiny eel

Deep sea shrimp

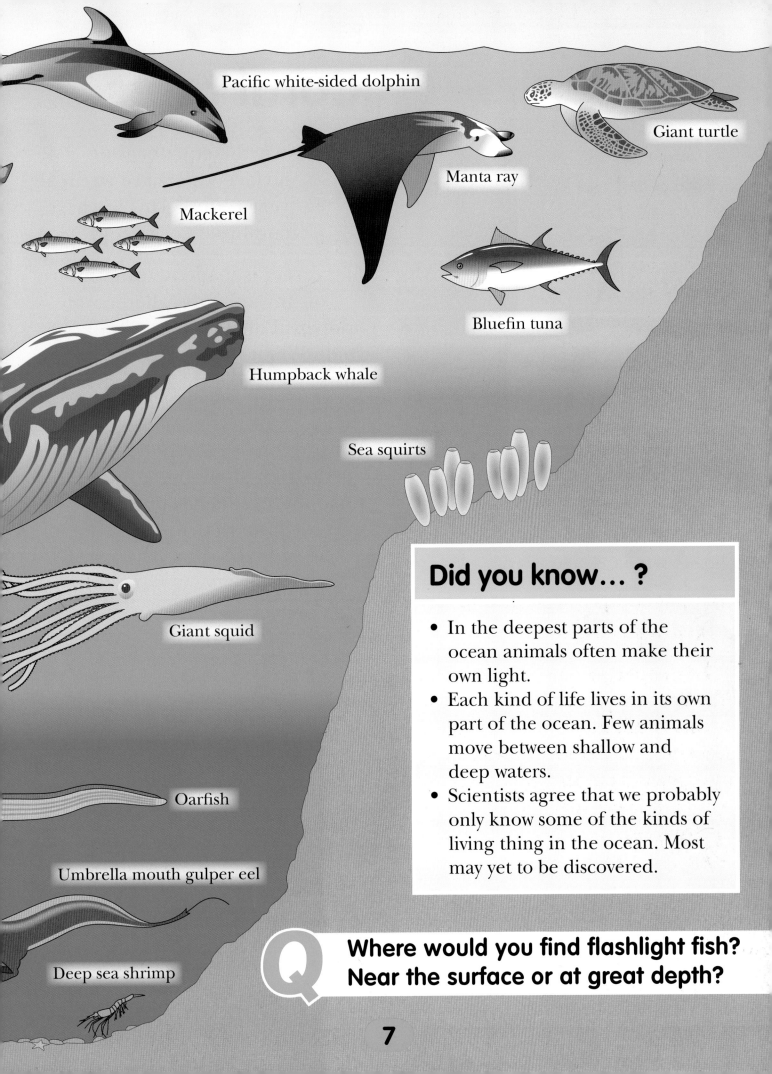

Pacific white-sided dolphin

Giant turtle

Manta ray

Mackerel

Bluefin tuna

Humpback whale

Sea squirts

Giant squid

Oarfish

Umbrella mouth gulper eel

Deep sea shrimp

Did you know… ?

- In the deepest parts of the ocean animals often make their own light.
- Each kind of life lives in its own part of the ocean. Few animals move between shallow and deep waters.
- Scientists agree that we probably only know some of the kinds of living thing in the ocean. Most may yet to be discovered.

Q **Where would you find flashlight fish? Near the surface or at great depth?**

Coral reefs

Near the equator the surface waters are warm all year round. This is where coral **reefs** can grow.

A reef is made up of millions of tiny animals called coral **polyps**. Polyps live in a kind of shell. When the polyps die, the shell remains and forms part of the coral reef.

During the day the polyps stay inside their shell, but at night they poke their **tentacles** out and wait for food to drift by.

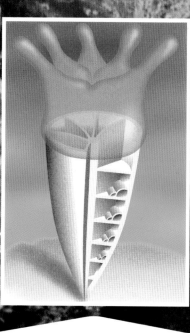

What a coral looks like. The pink part is soft and alive, the white part is old skeletons (coral rock).

Did you know… ?

- There are two types of coral. Hard corals (like brain coral and elkhorn coral) have hard skeletons which form coral reefs. Soft corals (like sea fingers and sea whips) do not build reefs.
- The Great Barrier Reef (off the coast of NE Australia) is the largest coral reef in the world. It is over 2,000 km long.
- Some of the oldest reefs today began growing over 25 million years ago.

Coral polyps are like barnacles: they must have something to fix themselves to. So they only grow in shallow, rocky water. If the water is muddy the polyps get all clogged up, so they only grow in clear waters, away from where rivers reach the sea.

Thousands of polyps grow together to make a colony, and millions of colonies make a reef. Young corals attach themselves to the skeletons of older corals and so the reef continually grows outwards.

Corals grow in many shapes and colours. The 'feathery' parts are the tentacles of polyps waving about in the water in search of food.

Q **Why do rivers stop corals from growing?**

Threats to reef life

Reefs are home for countless thousands of types of living things. For example, four thousand **species** of fish (nearly a fifth of all living fish) live close to coral reefs.

What makes it such an attractive home? Reefs offer many nooks and crannies for small fish to hide in.

Of course, lots of small fish are the food that larger fish are looking for, so the reef is also a hunting ground of sharks, groupers, octopuses and others.

The corals themselves are food for parrotfish, sea stars and other creatures.

A number of animals live in the coral itself, either boring into the limestone surface or living in the nooks and crannies. They include sponges and mussels.

Turtle with Butterfly fish.

Q Why are these fish keeping close to the reef?

The cold ocean

The Southern Ocean couldn't be more different to the tropical seas where corals live. It reaches around the frozen continent of Antarctica. Winds regularly reach over gale force and waves can be huge. Water temperatures are as low as −1.8°C and giant icebergs are common.

Can anything live in such terrifyingly harsh conditions? In fact, the Southern Ocean is one of the richest seas in the world. Its depths contain huge shoals of fish and squid, which in turn provide food for large numbers of birds, seals and whales.

The cold oceans are most full of life in the summer (December and January). During these months there is almost 24 hours of daylight, and the water is warm enough to allow the growth of tiny **microscopic** creatures called **plankton**.

Plankton are eaten by shrimp-like creatures called krill. The krill usually live in vast swarms, with more than 10,000 in each cubic metre of water. There are so many, that when they shoal near the surface their bodies make the sea look red.

Krill are a vital part of the food chain in many oceans.

12

Did you know… ?

- The word krill is Norwegian, meaning 'whale food'.
- Fish living in the Southern and Arctic Oceans have antifreeze in their veins.
- The emperor penguin stands up to 1.2 m tall and weighs up to 41 kilos.
- Male emperor penguins hold their eggs on their feet all winter long, huddled together in groups of thousands for warmth.
- The cold ocean food chain is very simple. If we over-fish krill, all creatures above them in the food chain will die.

Birds (such as gulls, terns, albatross and penguins), squid, octopus, many kinds of fish, seals and whales eat the krill.

Leopard seals, sperm and killer whales then eat the penguins, squid, octopus and seals.

Q **What kind of creatures are krill?**

Underwater forests and meadows

All life on Earth depends on plants. This is as true below the sea as above it. Most ocean plants are too small to be seen. They float about in the oceans and are called plankton. But oceans are also home to many grasses and **seaweeds**. One important shallow-water seaweed is called kelp. Kelp fasten themselves to rocky surfaces with 'holdfasts', then grow up to the surface, where they spread out, making a 'canopy forest'.

The kelp forest is home to many animals. For example, slugs, snails and many similar creatures graze on the leaves (called blades). Small fish seek shelter in the stems (called fronds) and octopus, cuttlefish, king crabs, seahorses and large fish move through the forest in search of small fish to eat. Thousands of other creatures – such as brittle stars, sea stars, anemones and sponges live on the holdfast.

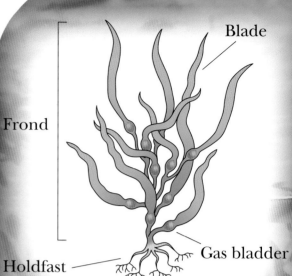

The features of kelp.

Seahorses looking for food and sheltering from larger creatures that might eat them.

Did you know… ?

- The largest seaweed in the world is the giant kelp. It reaches 54 m long and grows 30 cm a day.
- Some kelp can stretch up to one and a half times its length, which helps it to avoid breaking in large waves.
- Pieces of dead kelp sink to the depths of the ocean and are eaten as food by deep sea creatures.
- The Sargasso Sea is home to the world's largest area of floating seaweeds.

Why do seahorses live in the kelp forest?

Whales, dolphins and seals

Whales, dolphins, porpoises, seals, sea lions, walruses, dugongs and sea otters are examples of **mammals**. These are animals that give milk to their young and breath air through their lungs.

Many mammals call the ocean home. These mammals have developed amazing ways to adapt to life in the water. Many have thick layers of fat, called **blubber**, to help them keep warm in the cold water.

Some ocean mammals, such as whales, dolphins and porpoises spend their whole lives in the water. They come up to the surface to breath and can take in enough air to spend more than an hour underwater.

Sea otters are unique because they don't have blubber. Instead, their fur is more dense than any other mammal, with up to one million hairs per square inch. Ten times more than you have on your head!

Seals, sea lions and walruses spend most of their lives swimming and eating in the water, but they come onto land or ice to bear their young, sunbathe and moult.

Dugongs and manatees live in shallow waters and eat plants.

Dolphins often jump clear out of the water. Scientists think this is often just for fun.

Did you know...?

- The northern elephant seal is capable of diving to depths of over 500 m and can remain under the surface of the water for 2 hours.
  - Blue whales are so large that a small person could crawl through their main arteries, and 20 people could stand on their tongue!

A humpback whale breaking the surface to refill its lungs with air.

Sirens are legendary Greek 'mermaids' that lured sailors to their death into the sea. Some people think that these legends came from sailors mistaking sea cows for humans with tails.

Did you know… ?

- Sharks are fish, but the skeleton of the shark is very different from that of bony fish such as cod; it is made from **cartilage** – the same as the stuff that makes up your ears – which is very light and flexible.
- Like other fish, sharks get oxygen from seawater as it passes over their gills. Because of their size and the fact that they move swiftly, many sharks need a lot more oxygen for their size than other fish. If these sharks were to stop swimming, they would not be able to move enough oxygen through their gills and they would suffocate.

Q **Why do sharks never stop swimming?**

There are over 370 different types of shark and the largest one feeds only on tiny plankton!

Sharks

Sharks are some of the world's most misunderstood creatures. For example, they very rarely attack humans unless threatened.

Many sharks eat fish. They often hunt around reefs where there are a lot of fish. Normally, sharks eat alone. But sometimes one feeding shark attracts others. They swim up as quickly as possible and all begin to try to get a piece of the **prey**. They bite wildly at anything that gets in their way – even each other. This is called a feeding frenzy.

One of the reasons that meat-eating sharks are successful is that they have such super senses. Two-thirds of a shark's brain is dedicated to its keenest sense – smell.

Not all sharks are fierce meat eaters. Some are quite harmless. Oddly enough, the most harmless sharks tend to be the largest! The basking shark and the whale shark (front cover picture) fit this description. These huge sharks eat plankton and krill.

Life with a soft body

Whales have a backbone, so do sharks and fish. But many types of animal do not have a skeleton inside. In the oceans they include jellyfish, sea anemone, sea worms, all shellfish, squids, octopuses, sponges and starfish.

Jellyfish drift over hundreds of kilometres driven by tides and currents. Sponges, by contrast, live most of their lives anchored to just one place.

Sea anemones look almost like flowers. They open out and wave their tentacles about until they feel an animal. Then they sting the animal, paralysing it. The tentacles then take the prey to the mouth where it is digested.

Sea anemones waving their colourful tentacles in search of food.

A sea slug grazing on algae on the ocean floor.

What does a sea anemone use its tentacles for?

Life in a shell

If you look along a beach you will often find **shells**. There are over 112,000 different species of sea creatures with shells. The shells come in a wide variety of shapes and sizes. Animals with shells include snails, clams and also octopuses (see page 24).

Many shellfish live in shallow water. Some bury themselves in the sand of a beach, others attach themselves to rocks and some even attach themselves to other animals.

Shellfish use their shells to support their bodies and also as protection.

Many shellfish have two parts (called valves) to their shells. Strong muscles attach themselves to the shells, allowing the animal to open and close the shells.

Shellfish have long tubes called siphons that reach into the water. They suck water in through one siphon, filter out any food and then send the water out through the other siphon.

Some also have a large foot which they use to move about on the sea bed.

Siphons

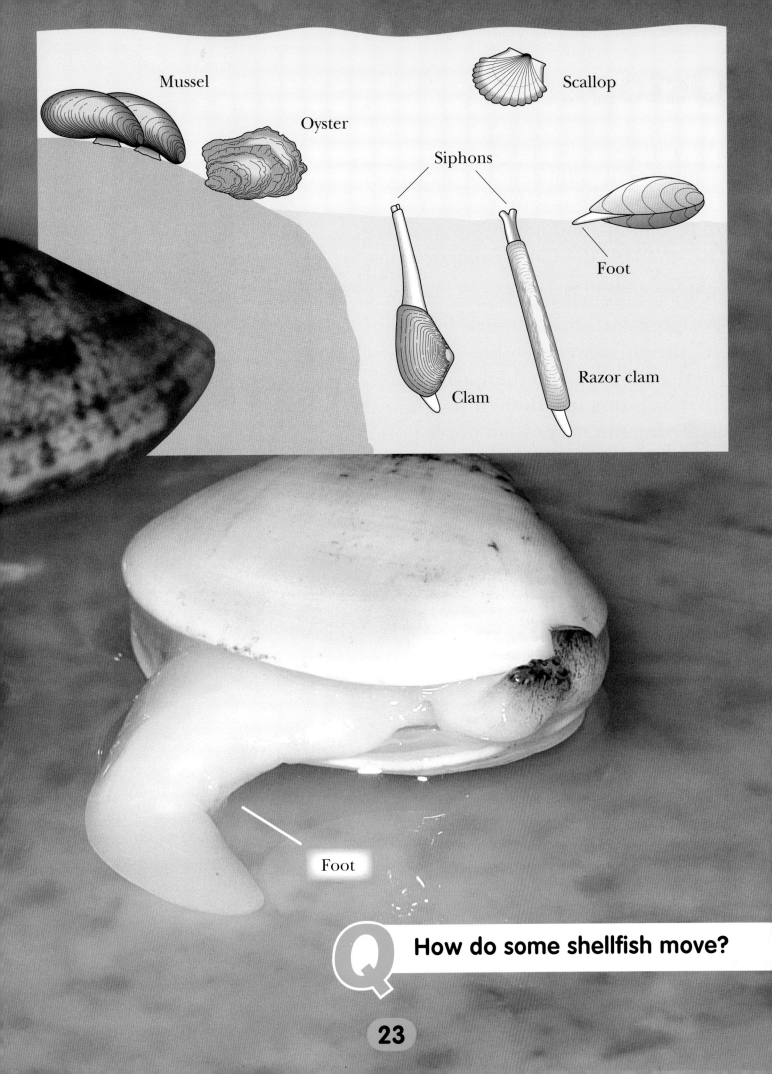

Mussel

Scallop

Oyster

Siphons

Foot

Clam

Razor clam

Foot

Q How do some shellfish move?

Octopuses

The word octopus means 'eight feet'. Octopuses live alone on the ocean floor. The giant octopus is up to 7 m from arm tip to arm tip, and weighs up to 200 kg. The smallest, the Californian octopus, is a mere 1 cm long.

Octopuses eat small animals like crabs and shrimp as well as other octopuses. They catch prey with their arms, then kill it by biting it with their tough beak, paralysing the prey with a nerve poison, and softening the flesh. Octopuses hunt mostly at night.

Octopuses live in small caves and under rocks. They pile rocks up to block the front of their den. The den protects them from being eaten by other animals like moray eels.

In order to escape from hunters, octopuses can squirt black ink into the water. They can also change their skin colour to blend into the background. The octopus swims by sending out a jet of water from its body.

Each arm has two rows of suction cups. It has blue blood. An octopus has an eye on each side of its head and has very good eyesight. An octopus cannot hear.

Octopuses are a favourite food in many countries.

Did you know... ?

- The Australian blue-ringed octopus has a poison strong enough to kill a person, but no others do.
- If an octopus loses an arm, it will regrow another one.
- Inside an octopus is a tiny shell, showing that it is related to animals with shells.

Q **What happens when an octopus loses an arm?**

Ocean birds

The oceans are a never-ending supply of food for countless millions of birds.

Some birds, like oyster catchers and avocets, wade in the surf at the sea's edge to catch food. Birds like gulls, pelicans and gannets plunge down from the air, diving to catch fish. A few of these, like the Arctic tern and wandering albatross, spend almost all their lives at sea. Some birds, like puffins and penguins, can swim for long periods underwater using their wings to 'fly' quickly after their prey.

The largest penguin is the emperor penguin, which grows to 1 m in height. The bigger kinds of penguin are best able to stand up to the cold, and so the bigger ones are found near the poles and the smaller ones nearer the tropics. Most penguins feed on krill, fish, squid and other forms of sea life caught while swimming underwater.

Puffins fly out to the open sea, then dive into the water to catch fish. Their short wings are adapted for swimming. They use a kind of flying technique under water. In the air, they often fly low over the ocean's surface, beating their wings at up to 100 times per minute.

Q Why are many birds found near breaking waves?

Gulls are closely related to the terns, but they will eat a greater range of foods, including food that humans put out for them or leave about as rubbish. Unlike terns, gulls are not afraid of humans. Because they can be **scavengers** they do well around humans when other birds are losing their feeding grounds.

Terns are common seabirds with white and grey feathers and a black head. Each year the Arctic tern makes an amazing journey from its breeding ground in the Arctic to its summer grounds in Antarctica. It literally travels around the world each year. An Arctic tern may live to be 20 years old. It eats fish, small clams, crabs and similar creatures.

Pollution and the ocean

Water is amazing. More substances can dissolve in water than any other liquid. But this does, of course, mean that if any kind of poison gets into the water, it will spread out quickly and reach a large area. As most ocean animals breathe by taking in water through their gills, this can have terrible results. Common poisons include fertilisers from farmland that get into the sea from rivers and waste pipes from factories that are emptied into the sea.

Sewage dumped at sea can create its own problems. It is very rich in food that tiny plants called algae use to grow. So they multiply greatly, using all the oxygen from the water and turning the water green (we call this an algal bloom). This also cuts off light to the lower parts of the ocean and so many creatures living under the algal bloom die.

Millions of water birds die every year due to oil from major oil spills, but also due to such seemingly harmless sources as motorboats. When a bird swims into oil on the surface of the water, the oil sticks to its feathers, causing them to matt and separate. As a result, water and cold can get to their sensitive skins. To deal with this, the bird tries to get the oil off its feathers by preening, and of course, in the process, the bird swallows the oil, which then poisons it.

When an oil tanker becomes damaged in stormy seas, it is often holed below the water line. As a result, oil seeps out. Many tankers carry crude oil, which is oil straight out of the ground. The heavy tarry part of the oil spreads out over the sea bed, smothering the clams, and other bottom-living creatures. The lighter part of the oil floats on the surface, where birds then swim or dive into it.

Beach

Oil slick

Tar balls

Ship holed?

Try these ...

Make a drawing of an ocean

- Make a drawing showing a side-on view of an ocean. Choose which plants and animals you want to draw, then put them in their proper places. Make sure you have some floating life, some shallow living life, some middle depth life and some deepwater life. Don't forget the life that lives on the ocean floor.

- Make sure all of your creatures live in the same kind of ocean. Don't, for example, put penguins (from cold water areas) in the same drawing as coral reefs (from tropical areas).

Make a classroom mural

- This can be a whole class activity or it can fill one wall of your bedroom if you want to do it yourself.
- This time simply choose the living things that you like best. Find pictures of them and cut them up.
- Then put the pictures on the wall using blu-tac or something else that can be pulled off without harming the wall surface.
- Write a description of each creature and stick that next to its picture.
- Photograph the whole thing and keep it as a reminder of the project you did.

Web sites change, but these existed when the book was printed. They have lots of pictures:

> http://www.seasky.org/sea.html
> http://www.photolib.noaa.gov/

Find out about overfishing

One of the big threats to the oceans is that people catch more and more fish. At some point more fish are taken than are born and fish become endangered. This is happening in the North Sea, the Atlantic and elsewhere. Find out about overfishing using the Internet. Here are some links:

en.wikipedia.org/wiki/Overfishing

http://www.yptenc.org.uk/docs/factsheets/env_facts/overfishing.htmlclassroom display.

Make an ocean exploration timeline

- Who explored the ocean, and when did they do it?
- Use the Internet to find out as many dates as you can, then make a timeline with them. Don't forget to add pictures to your timeline if you can find them.
- Don't forget you can find out about ocean explorers such as Sir Walter Raleigh (from your History/Tudors course) as well as underwater explorers like Jacques Cousteau.

Glossary

algae Simple, usually tiny, plant-like creatures that live in water. They capture light energy and use it to make their tissues.

blubber A thick layer of fat that is loosely attached to the rest of the body. It forms an insulating blanket against the cold of the ocean.

cartilage A soft, fibrous material that can connect bones and can also make what looks at first like a skeleton.

mammal Warm-blooded creatures that feed their young with milk.

microscopic Something that is too small to be seen except with powerful lenses.

ocean The great mass of connected saltwaters that cover nearly three quarters of the surface of the Earth.

plankton Tiny, often microscopic, creatures that drift with the ocean waters. Some are plants, others are animals.

polyp Simple soft-bodied creatures that are long, jelly-like tubes.

prey An animal that is food for a hunter.

reef A rock or sandbar lying just beneath the surface of the water.

scavengers Animals that eat the dead remains of other animals.

seaweeds Large forms of algae, such as kelp.

shell A hard protective curved plate that surrounds animals known as molluscs.

species A group of creatures which can breed with one another.

tentacles Long, movable organs used for grasping and feeding. They are longer than arms and usually have suckers at their tips only (octopuses do not have tentacles: they have arms).

Index

albatross **13, 26**
algae **11, 14–15, 28, 32**
Antarctica **12**
cartilage **18, 32**
clam **22–23**
coral **8–11**
dolphin **7, 16, 17**
dugong **16, 17**
eel **7, 24**
Great Barrier Reef **8, 21**
gull **13, 26, 27**
iceberg **12**
jellyfish **20**
kelp **14–15**
krill **12–13, 19, 26**
mammal **16–17, 32**

Mariana Trench **4**
microscopic creatures **12, 32**
mussel **10, 22–23**
octopus **10, 13, 14, 22, 24-25**
oil pollution **28–29**
oyster **23**
penguin **13, 26, 28–29**
plankton **12, 14, 19, 32**
pollution **28–29**
polyp **8–9, 32**
prey **19, 32**
puffin **27**
reef **1, 5, 8–11, 21**
Sargasso Sea **15**

scallop **23**
scavenger **27, 32**
sea anemone **14, 20–21**
sea cow **17**
sea horse **15**
seal **13, 16, 17**
seaweed **14–15, 32**
sewage **28**
shark **1, 6, 10, 18–19**
shell **22, 25, 32**
shellfish **22–23**
Southern Ocean **12**
species **10, 21, 22, 32**
sponge **10, 14, 20**
tentacles **8, 9, 20, 32**
tern **13, 27**
turtle **10, 11**
whale **7, 13, 16–17, 20**

Curriculum Visions

Curriculum Visions is a registered trademark of Atlantic Europe Publishing Company Ltd.

Atlantic Europe Publishing

Curriculum Visions Explorers
This series provides straightforward introductions to key worlds and ideas.

You might also be interested in
'Exploring the threatened rainforest', 'Exploring climate chaos' and 'Caring for our environment'. Teacher's Notes in PDF format are also available from the publisher to support 'Exploring the threatened oceans'. All of these products are suitable for KS2.

Dedicated Web Site
Watch movies, see many more pictures and read much more in detail about oceans and caring for our environment at:

www.curriculumvisions.com
(Professional Zone: subscription required)

First published in 2007 by Atlantic Europe Publishing Company Ltd
Copyright © 2007 Earthscape

Author
Brian Knapp, BSc, PhD

Educational Consultant
JM Smith (former Deputy Head of Wellfield School, Burnley, Lancashire)

Senior Designer
Adele Humphries, BA

Editor
Gillian Gatehouse

Photographs
The Earthscape Picture Library, except Rick Frehsee, Blackbeard's Cruises, Bahamas cover; IFAW International Fund for Animal Welfare/J. Hrusa www.ifaw.org p28–29; NASA p4 (inset); Richard Seaman p12–13; ShutterStock p1, 2–3, 4–5, 8–9, 10–11, 13 (insets), 14–15, 16–17, 18–19, 20–21, 22–23, 24–25, 26–27, 30–31.

Illustrations
David Woodroffe

Designed and produced by
Earthscape

Printed in China by
WKT Company Ltd

Exploring the threatened oceans – Curriculum Visions
A CIP record for this book is available from the British Library
ISBN 978 1 86214 211 4

This product is manufactured from sustainable managed forests. For every tree cut down at least one more is planted.